HOW TO USE A CAPO
FOR GUITAR

by John Tapella

Research by Nina de Rochemont

ISBN 978-0-7935-8819-0

HAL•LEONARD®
CORPORATION

7777 W. BLUEMOUND RD. P.O. BOX 13819 MILWAUKEE, WI 53213

Visit Hal Leonard Online at
www.halleonard.com

TABLE OF
CONTENTS

CHAPTER 1

WHAT IS A CAPO?

Capo, Capotasto *(Italian, KAH-poh [or KAY-poh], kah-poh-TAH-stoh)* **1:** The head, beginning, nut, or top. **2:** On string instruments, a device placed around the fingerboard that raises the pitch of the strings.

The Capo

A capo generally consists of a metal rod with one rubber side and an elastic strap; the rubber side lies flat against all six strings while the strap wraps around the back of the guitar neck, behind the frets. The capo allows you to play first-position chords in all keys by moving it from fret to fret. The most common keys played using a capo are: E, B, A, G, D, and C. Another advantage of the capo is that you can play open strings on any fret you place it. For example, by placing the capo on the fifth fret, you can play a D chord form on the seventh fret with an open fourth string. The capo may also be used for chords with wide stretches and leads. Part of the chord can be played on the higher frets, while the other notes may be played on the capoed fret.

Partial Capoing

You may also use a capo on selected strings, leaving the others open. This technique is called *partial capoing* and is useful if your music involves experimental sounds and chords.

Capo Facts

- Classical and jazz guitar music generally do not use the capo, although flamenco music makes extensive use of it.

- Guitars made before the 1950s have thicker necks and require the U-shaped or clamped capo to fit their larger necks.

- Adjustable thumb-screw capos allow you to fine tune the pressure on the strings. These capos are handy because they are less likely to wear down the strings or frets and upset the tuning. The downside of the thumb-screw capo is it takes longer to adjust.

- Some capos are designed to rest on the head of the guitar or below the nut when not in use. This type of capo is useful if you play live and have a set with only some capoed songs. After playing a song with the capo, you can quickly adjust it to rest on the neck and don't have to completely remove it.

- A homemade capo may be made from a pencil, a few inches of string, and a heavy rubber band.

- Be careful not to hit the capo while playing, as it may throw your guitar out of tune.

- Elastic capos fit most guitars, even National steel guitars. The double elastic or heavy elastic type use a soft rubber. These capos are best for 12-string guitars as they mold with the strings. On a 12-string guitar, the strings are closer together and require a capo that won't pull on the strings. Elastic stretch capos are simple in design and keep their shape after months of use.

Capo Types

Shubb Capo

The Shubb capo is a C-clamp capo with an added piece of brass that lies flat across the strings and curves under the neck. Attached to this is a hinged piece with a thumb screw that holds the capo in place. By pivoting the metal bar, the hinged piece applies pressure to the neck and locks into place. Some of the advantages of this capo are that the thumb screw regulates pressure on the strings, replacement rubber pieces are available, and a capo clip can be bought so you can attach the capo to a belt or your guitar neck.

Trigger Capo by Dunlop

The Trigger capo is designed like the trigger of a gun and can be manipulated with one hand. It has a ridged grip handle with clamping spring action. By squeezing the gripped handle, the center piece opens and can be clamped on the guitar neck when released. The disadvantage of this capo is that it does not have precise control over the pressure on the strings as thumb-screw capos do.

Bird of Paradise Capo by Digital Revolution

The Bird of Paradise capo is made of plastic, and designed like a wrench or bird's beak. It grips evenly across the strings and doesn't throw your guitar out of tune. It is widely adjustable and fits narrow, wide, flat, and curved necks. It easily clips to the head of your guitar when not being used.

Glider Capo by THREE CC

The Glider capo is made with two metal circular rollers in a C-clamp shape. One spring is attached to each roller. The top roller has a rectangular-shaped rubber piece that lies against the strings; the bottom roller has an hourglass piece of rubber that clamps against the back of the neck, holding the capo in place. The Glider is useful on both acoustic and electric guitars and can be easily moved up and down the neck, even during a song.

Bill Russell Type

Elastic capos are the least expensive model, but also have a tendency to wear out more quickly than other models. Elastic capos are made of a jagged metal rod with a soft rubber side, which faces the strings, and an elastic band. The elastic band has small holes that hook onto the jagged metal rod at different lengths. These models come with thin elastic bands (not recommended), heavy elastic bands, or double elastic bands.

Third Hand Capo

The Third Hand capo is designed like the Russell capo, but it enables you to capo specific strings. The main section is divided into six rubber sections that can be individually pushed onto the strings, letting you choose which strings you want capoed. For example, place the capo on the second fret, covering only the first four strings. Then hold the first string, fifth fret note A, while strumming from the fifth string down. You are now playing a capoed A chord with an open fifth string! This capo is ideal for experimenting with new and inventive chord shapes and is probably best for intermediate and advanced guitarists.

Jim Dunlop Capo

Jim Dunlop makes a capo with a flat metal and rubber piece that presses against the strings and a nylon band that wraps around the neck to hold the capo in place. The nylon band attaches to the metal piece and may be adjusted for varying tightness and for different widths along the neck. These capos are small and last a long time. However, they tend to fly open.

Clamp Style or U-Shape

The clamp style or U-shape capo is made of a flat piece of metal with a hard rubber lining which is attached to a metal U-shaped clamp that fits under and behind the neck. The metal parts are tightened with a thumb screw. Thumb screw capos allow precise pressure on the strings. These capos lock in place, creating great sound, but are time consuming to move around the neck. I've listed four types of U-shaped capos on the next page.

1 *Baldy U Capo*

The Baldy U capo is made of thin stainless steel and employs a thumb screw to tighten in place. It is one of the least visible capos. Unfortunately, it does not usually fit on thick-necked guitars.

2 *Paige U Capo*

The Paige U capo is made of stainless steel or brass and also has a thumb screw design. This capo can also have trouble fitting thick-necked guitars.

3 *Saga Capo*

Saga capos are U shaped and made of brass. Most Saga capos fit thick-necked guitars.

4 Picker's Pal

The Picker's Pal capo is a U-shaped capo similar to the thumb screw models except it has a plastic lever for tightening the capo in place instead of a thumb screw. The lever can be tightened or released with one motion, making it easy to attach and detach quickly, whereas the thumb screw models may take several turns to release or tighten. The Picker's Pal capo also has a rectangular metal top with four different types of rubber surfaces to choose from. You have only to rotate the metal top piece to select the rubber surface which best suits the strings and guitar you are playing.

Victor Capo

The Victor capo is an unusual, V-shaped capo. Made of brass, this capo has an adjustable thumb screw at the bottom end of the V. This capo fits on the side of the guitar neck, instead of adjusting underneath the neck of the guitar. The thumb screw tightens or loosens the side of the V that fits the back of the guitar neck. This capo is durable, has the advantage of fine tuning like other thumb screw models, and is easily adjustable with one hand. But it, too, has trouble fitting thick-necked guitars.

Kyser Capo

The Kyser capo rarely fits the older and thicker-necked guitars. It has a flat T-shaped metal piece with slightly curled edges. The shaft of the T shape is what is used to apply pressure to the strings. One half of the T's top end curls downward and is attached to a rubber-covered metal piece with a strong spring. This part is designed to hug the neck of the guitar. The other half of the T's top curls upwards, making it easier to grasp and squeeze the spring that opens the capo for placement on the guitar neck.

Capo Notation

Wherever the capo is placed becomes "0" in TAB. All TAB numbers will be counted from the capo. Key signature, notation, and chord names will reflect the sound relative to the

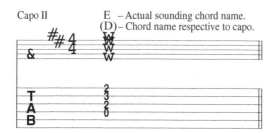

capo, not the actual sounding pitch.

Fig. 1

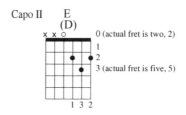

Chord diagrams will be counted from the capo.

Editor's note: Use alternate picking throughout, except for chords in succession—then use downstrokes.

CAPO STYLES

Indigo Girls Style

These examples demonstrate basic chord shapes with several different chord-rhythm patterns. Substitute the different rhythms on these chord progressions.

Fig. 3

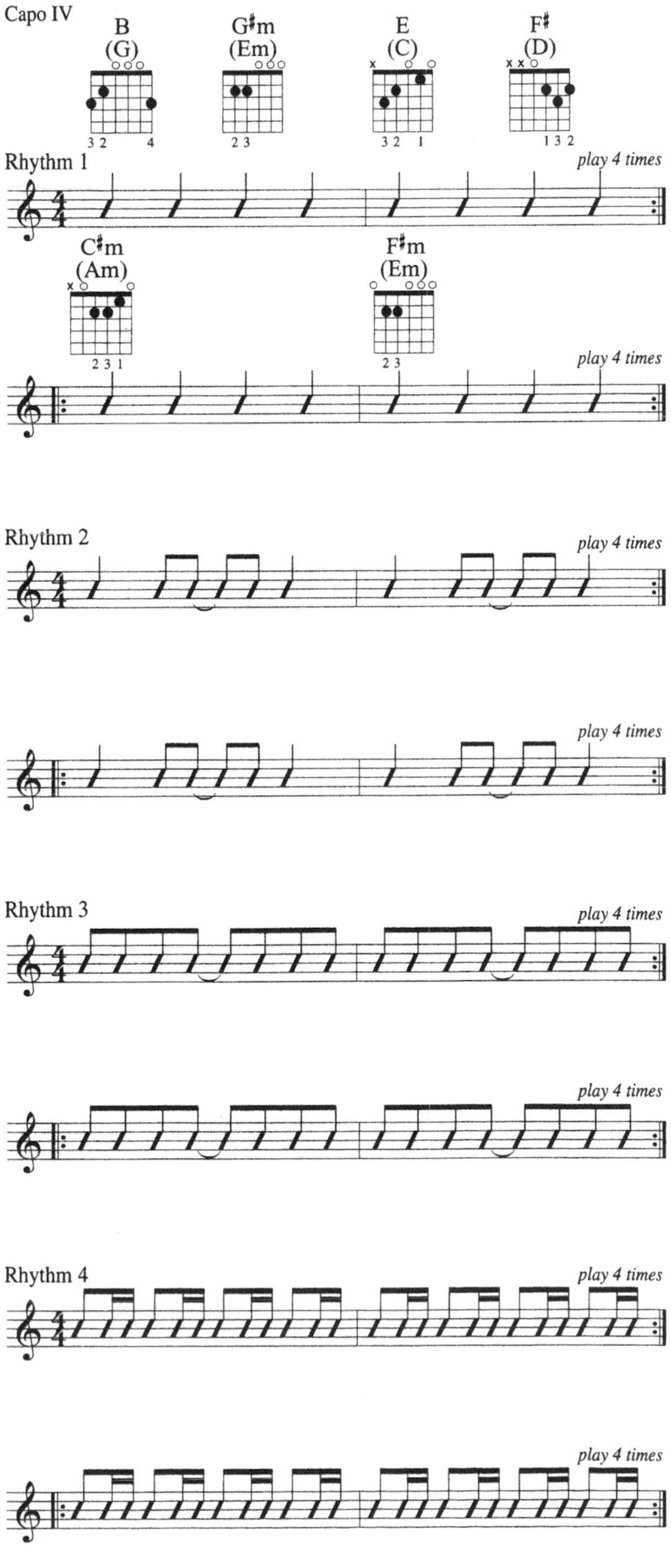

Fig. 4

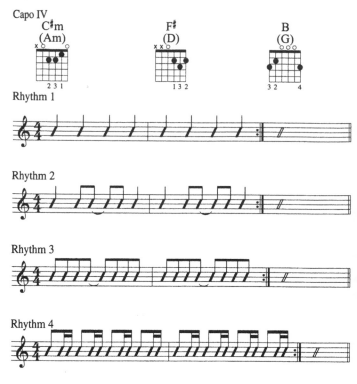

Capo IV

C#m (Am) F# (D) B (G)

Rhythm 1

Rhythm 2

Rhythm 3

Rhythm 4

Sixties Style

Play this exercise with an E minor chord and descending bass line. The E minor chord remains stationary while the bass line descends from E(D) to D(C) to Db(B) to a C7(Bb7) chord and then a B(A) chord.

Fig. 5

Capo II

Moderately Slow ♩ = 90

Em *(Dm)   Em/D (Dm/C)

let ring

*Symbols in parentheses represent chord names respective to capoed guitar. Symbols above reflect actual sounding chord.

Em/Db (Dm/B)   C7 (Bb7)

B (A)   Bsus4 (Asus4)

George Harrison-Style Arpeggios

This example uses basic chord shapes played in *arpeggios* (chord tones played in single note sequences) and adds suspensions to the A (D) and E7(A7) arpeggios. These suspensions consist of the root, fifth, and added fourth.

Fig. 6

Capo VII

*Symbols in parentheses represent chord names respective to capoed guitar.
Symbols above reflect actual sounding chord.

Country-Style Capo

This country riff plays an A(G) chord with the second, third, and fourth strings open, and a D(C) chord with the third string open. The riffs are played with the A(G) major pentatonic, E(D) Mixolydian, and D(C) major scales.

Fig. 7

Capo II   A   A major pentatonic
        *(G) (G major pentatonic)

*Symbols in parentheses represent chord names respective to capoed guitar. Symbols above reflect actual sounding chord.

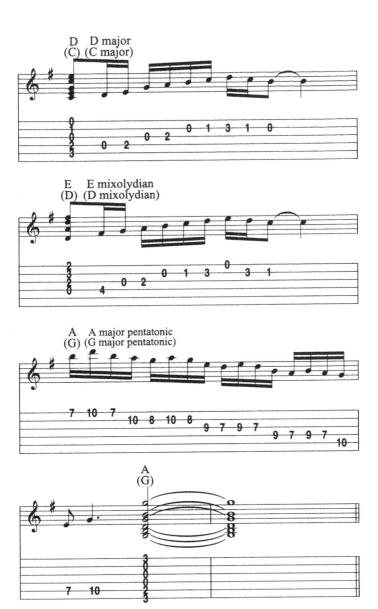

Joan Osborne (Fingerpicking) Style

Play these chord forms with a fingerpicking style. The melody notes are struck upward with your right hand middle finger while the bass notes are struck downward with the pick held between your right hand thumb and index finger.

Fig. 8

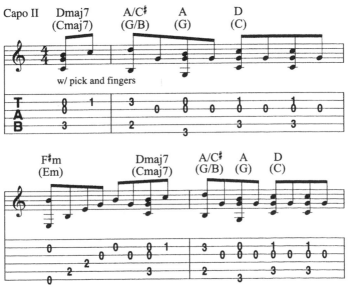

Triplets/Descending Bass

This example is played with triplets on the first, second, and third beats of measures 1, 2, and 3. Measure 3 ends the example with a descending bass line leading to the final G(D) chord in measure 4.

Fig. 9

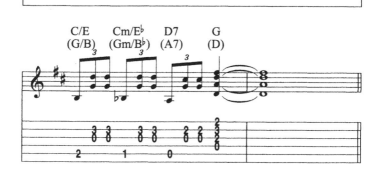

CAPO TUNINGS

Drop-D Bass

This example is in Drop-D tuning (tune your sixth string down one whole step to D) and sounds the sixth string low F (D) bass note every two beats in measures 1-4, and 7-9.

Fig. 10

Drop-D Tuning; Capo III:

① = E   ④ = D
② = B   ⑤ = A
③ = G   ⑥ = D

Byrds Style Drop-D Tuning

This example is in Drop-D tuning. The sixth string on your guitar is lowered one whole step while the remaining strings stay in standard tuning (low to high: D–A–D–G–B–E).

Fig. 11

Drop-D Tuning; Capo II:

① = E   ④ = D
② = B   ⑤ = A
③ = G   ⑥ = D

Keith Richards Style

To play in open G tuning, lower your first, fifth, and sixth strings down one whole step (low to high: D–G–D–G–B–D). Measure 1 begins with an E(B) to D(A) riff in two octaves and progresses to a D(A) minor seventh chord with a C(G) in the bass. In measure 2, D(A) minor seventh leads to a G5(D5) chord. Measure 3 starts with an open C(G) bass note on the first beat. Let this note ring while you move your left hand up to the tenth fret chord B♭(F) followed by F(C) on the eighth fret. Measure 4 transitions to a C(G) major pentatonic riff returning to a G5(D5) chord in measures 5 and 6. Measure 7 ends with a C(G) chord.

Fig. 12

Open G Tuning

In measure 1, descending two-note dyads outline a descending C♯(E) minor pentatonic scale leading to an open B5(G5) chord pattern in measure 2.

Fig. 13

Open G Tuning; Capo IV:
① = D ④ = D
② = B ⑤ = G
③ = G ⑥ = D

*sounded on repeat

Open G Tuning Chords

In measure 1, open B5(G5) chords lead to an E(C) chord (barred with your first finger on the fifth fret, across the second to fifth strings). Then an A/E (F/C) chord is formed on the and of beat 4 by dropping your second finger onto the second string, sixth fret and your third finger onto the fourth string, seventh fret while leaving your first finger barred across the fifth fret.

Fig. 14

Open G Tuning; Capo IV:
① = D ④ = D
② = B ⑤ = G
③ = G ⑥ = D

*Symbols in parentheses represent chord names respective to capoed guitar. Symbols above reflect actual sounding chord.

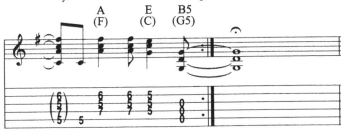

Robert Johnson Style

This example is played in 12/8 time, which is counted in sections of threes (1–2–3, 4–5–6, 7–8–9, 10–11–12). Your guitar is tuned to open G tuning (low to high: D–G–D–G–B–D) and a capo is placed on the second fret, raising the open G tuning up to A.

Fig. 15

Open G Tuning; Capo II:
① = D   ④ = D
② = B   ⑤ = G
③ = G   ⑥ = D

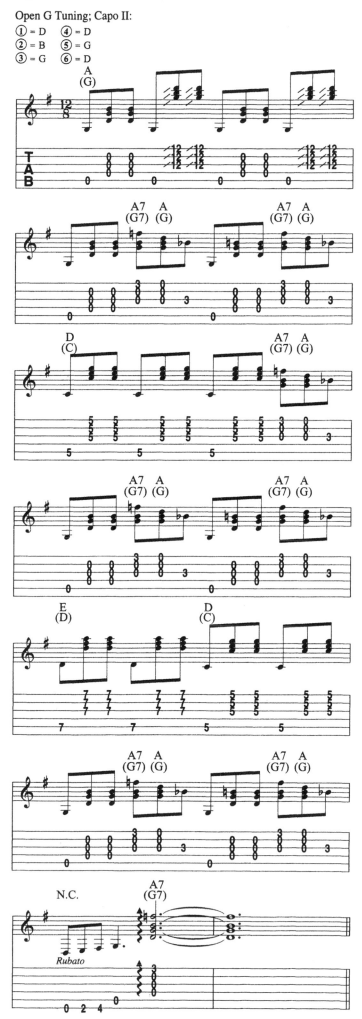

CHAPTER 4

CAPO CHORD SHAPES

Basic Capo Chord Shapes in Standard Tuning

These chord shapes are shown with a capo on the second fret, but may be moved up and down the neck along with the capo.

Fig. 16

Capo II

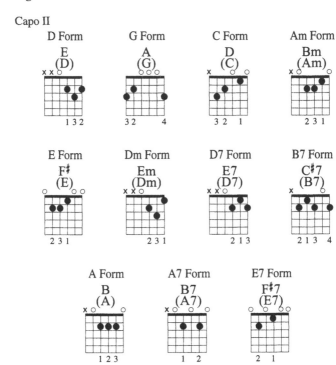

Standard Tuning Capo Shapes

Here are some less common chord forms you can use with a capo. These examples are shown with the capo on the third fret. See how they sound with the capo on other frets.

Fig. 17

Capo III

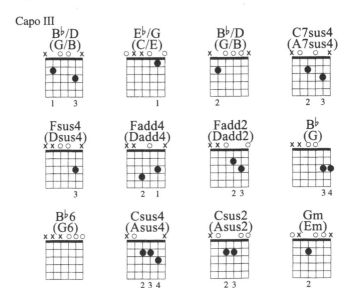

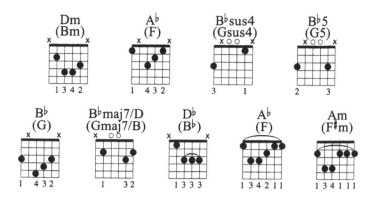

Try these four chords together. They all share the same two notes on top.

Fig. 18

Capo IV

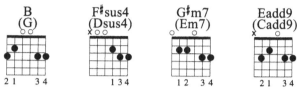

Try this group together. They share the same top notes with a walking bassline.

Fig. 19

Capo V

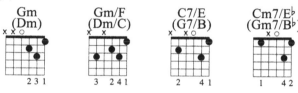

Now try these seven chords together. Do they sound familiar?

Fig. 20

Capo VII

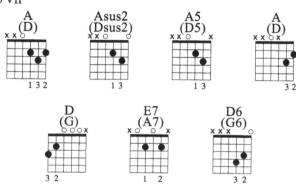

Drop-D Tuning Capo Shapes

Tune your sixth string down one whole step to D. The remaining strings stay in standard tuning. These examples are shown with the capo on the second fret. However, they can be used with the capo on any fret.

Fig. 21

Drop-D Tuning; Capo II:

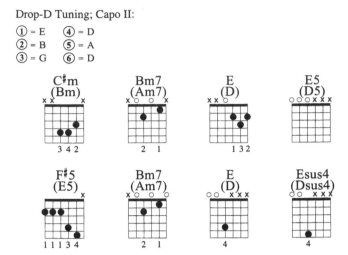

Open G Tuning Capo Shapes

Tune your guitar to open G (low to high: D–G–D–G–B –D). These examples are shown with the capo on the fourth fret, however they can be used with the capo on any fret. It is common to place the capo on the second fret, putting the guitar in "Open A tuning." See how these chords sound with the capo on other frets!

Fig. 22

Open G Tuning; Capo IV:

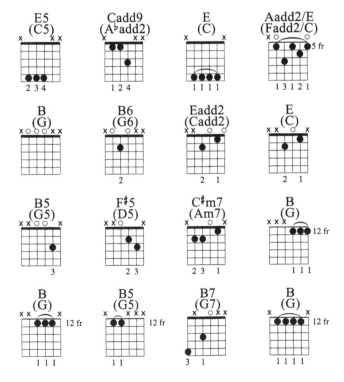

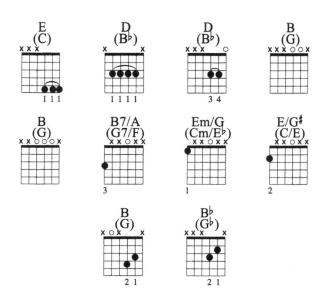

used with the capo on any fret.

Fig. 21

Open G Tuning Capo Shapes

Tune your guitar to open G (low to high: D–G–D–G–B–D). These examples are shown with the capo on the fourth fret, however they can be used with the capo on any fret. It is common to place the capo on the second fret, putting the guitar in "Open A tuning." See how these chords sound with the capo on other frets!

Fig. 22

Song	Artist	Capo/Tuning
"6th Avenue Heartache"	Wallflowers	Third Fret Standard
"Afternoons and Coffeespoons"	Crash Test Dummies	Third Fret Standard
"All For You"	Sister Hazel	First Fret Standard
"Aqualung"	Jethro Tull	Third Fret Standard
"Barangrill"	Joni Mitchell	First Fret D-A-C-F♯-A-D
"Bo Diddley"	Bo Diddley	Third Fret Standard
"Boom Boom"	John Lee Hooker	First Fret Standard
"Both Sides Now"	Joni Mitchell	Fourth Fret Open D
"Break in the Cup"	David Wilcox	Third Fret C-G-D-G-A-D
"Building a Mystery"	Sarah McLachlan	Second Fret E-A-D-G-B-D
"Casual Affair"	Tonic	Fourth Fret Open D9
"Cincinnati Jail"	Lonnie Mack	Third Fret Standard
"Down Child"	John Lee Hooker	First Fret Open A
"Fire and Rain"	James Taylor	Third Fret Standard
"Folsom Prison Blues"	Johnny Cash	First Fret Standard
"Free Falling"	Tom Petty	First Fret Standard 12-str.

Song	Artist	Capo/Tuning
"Go Your Own Way"	Fleetwood Mac *(Gtr. 1)*	Third Fret Open G
"Go Your Own Way"	Fleetwood Mac *(Gtr. 2)*	Fifth Fret Standard 12-str.
"Hammer and a Nail"	Indigo Girls	Fourth Fret Standard
"Happy"	The Rolling Stones	Fourth Fret Open G
"Here Comes the Sun"	The Beatles	Seventh Fret Standard
Song	**Artist**	**Capo/Tuning**
"Hey You"	Pink Floyd	Fifth Fret Standard
"Hold On"	Sarah McLachlan	Sixth Fret D-A-D-G-A-D
"Hotel California"	The Eagles	Seventh Fret Standard
"I Feel Lucky"	Mary Chapin Carpenter	Second Fret Standard
"I Don't Want to Wait"	Paula Cole	Second Fret Standard
"I Do"	Lisa Loeb	Third Fret Standard
"I'm Your Hoochie Coochie Man"	Muddy Waters	Fifth Fret Standard
"I've Got a Tiger By the Tail"	Buck Owens	Second Fret Standard
"Ice Pick"	Albert Collins	Seventh Fret Open Fm
"If You Could Only See"	Tonic	First Fret Standard
"If I Needed Someone"	The Beatles	Seventh Fret Standard
"Ironic"	Alanis Morissette	Fourth Fret Standard
"Jamie's Got a Gun"	Aerosmith	Second Fret Standard
"Let Her Cry"	Hootie and the Blowfish	Seventh Fret Standard
"Like a Rolling Stone"	The Rolling Stones	Fifth Fret Open G
"Little Sister"	Ry Cooder	Third Fret Open G
"Lost in the Here and Now"	Doug Smith	Second Fret D-G-D-G-A-E
"Lyin' Eyes"	The Eagles	Fifth Fret Standard
"Me and My Car"	Lonnie Mack	Third Fret

Song	Artist	Capo/Tuning
		Standard
"Me Wise Magic"	Van Halen	Second Fret Standard
"My Michelle"	The Beatles	Fifth Fret Standard
"Midnight Rambler"	The Rolling Stones	Seventh Fret Standard
"Mmm Mmm Mmm Mmm"	Crash Test Dummies	Third Fret Standard

Song	Artist	Capo/Tuning
"Never Going Back"	Lindsay Buckingham/ Fleetwood Mac	Fourth Fret C-G-D-G-B-E
"Night Moves"	Bob Segar	First Fret Standard
"Norwegian Wood"	The Beatles	Second Fret Standard
"Nowhere Man"	The Beatles	Second Fret Standard
"One of Us"	Joan Osborne	Second Fret Standard
"Only Wanna Be With You"	Hootie & the Blowfish	Second Fret Standard
"Past One O'Clock"	Robin Williamson	Third Fret C-A-D-A-A-E
"Place to Be"	Nick Drake	Second Fret D-A-D-G-A-F♯
"Renaissance Fair"	The Byrds	Third Fret Standard
"Rock and Roll Bones"	Lonnie Mack	Third Fret Standard
"Sally Mae"	John Lee Hooker	First Fret Open A
"Spiderwebs"	No Doubt	Third Fret Standard
"Take it to the Limit"	The Eagles	Fourth Fret Standard
"Tennessee Flat Top Box"	Roseanne Cash	First Fret Standard
"That Song About the Midway"	Joni Mitchell	Second Fret D-A-D-E-A-E
"That'll Be the Day"	Buddy Holly	Fifth Fret Standard
"That's What the Lonely Is For"	David Wilcox	Second Fret C-G-D-F♯-A-D
"The Freshmen"	Verve Pipe	Second Fret Standard

Song	Artist	Capo/Tuning
"The Difference"	The Wallflowers	Second Fret Down 1/2 step
"The Joker"	Steve Miller	Third Fret Standard
"The Three Sisters"	Muriel Anderson	Third Fret Drop-D
"The Earth Stopped Cold at Dawn"	Hootie and the Blowfish	Second Fret Standard
"Three Walls and a Bar"	Leo Kottke	Second Fret Drop-D
Song	**Artist**	**Capo/Tuning**
"Till I Hear it from You"	Gin Blossoms	Second Fret Standard
"Tavelin' Riverside Blues"	Robert Johnson	First Fret A Tuning
"Tumbling Dice"	The Rolling Stones	Second Fret Standard
"Wham"	Lonnie Mack	First Fret Standard
"While My Guitar Gently Weeps"	The Beatles	Fifth Fret Standard
"Wonderwall"	Oasis	Second Fret Standard
"Workin' Man Blues"	James Burton	Fourth Fret Standard
"You Learn"	Alanis Morissette	First Fret Standard
"You've Got a Friend"	James Taylor	Third Fret Standard

NOTATION

LEGEND

Guitar music can be notated three different ways: on a *musical staff*, in *tablature*, and in *rhythm slashes*.

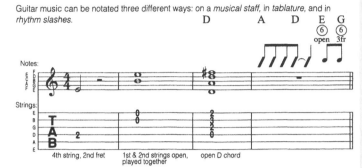

Notes:

Strings:

4th string, 2nd fret   1st & 2nd strings open,   open D chord
                       played together

RHYTHM SLASHES are written above the staff. Strum chords in the rhythm indicated. Use the chord diagrams found at the top of the first page of the transcription for the appropriate chord voicings. Round noteheads indicate single notes.

THE MUSICAL STAFF shows pitches and rhythms and is divided by bar lines into measures. Pitches are named after the first seven letters of the alphabet.

TABLATURE graphically represents the guitar fingerboard. Each horizontal line represents a string, and each number represents a fret.

HALF-STEP BEND: Strike the note and bend up 1/2 step.

WHOLE-STEP BEND: Strike the note and bend up one step.

GRACE NOTE BEND: Strike the note and bend up as indicated. The first note does not take up any time.

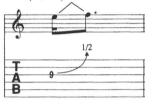

SLIGHT (MICROTONE) BEND: Strike the note and bend up 1/4 step.

BEND AND RELEASE: Strike the note and bend up as indicated, then release back to the original note. Only the first note is struck.

PRE-BEND: Bend the note as indicated, then strike it.

VIBRATO: The string is vibrated by rapidly bending and releasing the note with the fretting hand.

WIDE VIBRATO: The pitch is varied to a greater degree by vibrating with the fretting hand.

HAMMER-ON: Strike the first (lower) note with one finger, then sound the higher note (on the same string) with another finger by fretting it without picking.

PULL-OFF: Place both fingers on the notes to be sounded. Strike the first note and without picking, pull the finger off to sound the second (lower) note.

28

LEGATO SLIDE: Strike the first note and then slide the same fret-hand finger up or down to the second note. The second note s not struck.

SHIFT SLIDE: Same as legato slide, except the second note is struck.

TRILL: Very rapidly alternate between the notes indicated by continuously hammering on and pulling off.

TAPPING: Hammer ("tap") the fret indicated with the pick-hand index or middle finger and pull off to the note fretted by the fret hand.

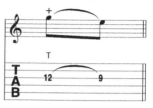

NATURAL HARMONIC: Strike the note while the fret-hand lightly touches the string directly over the fret indicated.

PITCH HARMONIC: The note is fretted normally and a harmonic is produced by adding the edge of the thumb or the tip of the index finger of the pick hand to the normal pick attack.

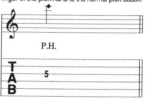

PICK SCRAPE: The edge of the pick is rubbed down (or up) the string, producing a scratchy sound.

MUFFLED STRINGS: A percussive sound is produced by laying the fret hand across the string(s) without depressing, and striking them with the pick hand.

PALM MUTE: The note is partially muted by the pick hand lightly touching the string(s) just before the bridge.

RAKE: Drag the pick across the strings indicated with a single motion.

TREMOLO PICKING: The note is picked as rapidly and continuously as possible.

VIBRATO BAR DIVE AND RETURN: The pitch of the note or chord is dropped a specified number of steps (in rhythm) then returned to the original pitch.

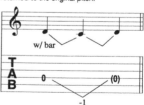

VIBRATO BAR SCOOP: Depress the bar just before striking the note, then quickly release the bar.

VIBRATO BAR DIP: Strike the note and then immediately drop a specified number of steps, then release back to the original pitch.